Let's Learn About Farm Machines

Tilling Equipment

Heather Moore Niver

Enslow Publishing
101 W. 23rd Street
Suite 240
New York, NY 10011
USA
enslow.com

Words to Know

blade The flat side of a tool or knife that is used for cutting.

crops Plants that are grown for food.

cultivating Getting the ground ready for planting or gardening.

fertilizer Material that is put into soil to help plants grow.

harvest To collect a crop.

herbicide A chemical used to get rid of weeds.

rotary Rotating; going around in a circle.

trench A long, narrow ditch or hole.

weed A plant that grows where it is not wanted.

CONTENTS

Soil must be tilled before farmers can plant crops.

What Is Tilling?

Farmers plant a lot of **crops**. Before they can plant, they have work to do. They have to get the soil ready. This is called **cultivating** or tilling.

Fast Fact
Tilling, or plowing, helps break up hard, chunky soil.

A tiller can tidy up a field that is full of weeds.

Tiller Talk: What Tillers Do

Tillers, or plows, move soil. They turn it over. Tillers also help mix **fertilizer** or bug killers into the dirt. Tillers help get rid of pesky **weeds**, too.

FAST FACT

Farmers can use fewer herbicides if they till.

Long ago, workers used simple hoes to prepare fields.

Dig It Up!

The first plows were simple. They were sticks! Farmers soon figured out a handle would be handy. Handles helped them move the stick better. Soon they added wheels and **blades**.

Fast Fact

A hoe was an early kind of hand tool for plowing.

A disk harrow system has many blades to break up the soil.

Digging the Disk Tiller

Disk tillers are great for hard or rocky soil. Disk tillers usually have lots of blades. They are sharp and plow deep. Some call them harrow or one-way disk plows.

FAST FACT

Plow is also spelled "plough."

A tractor pulls a large rotary tiller.

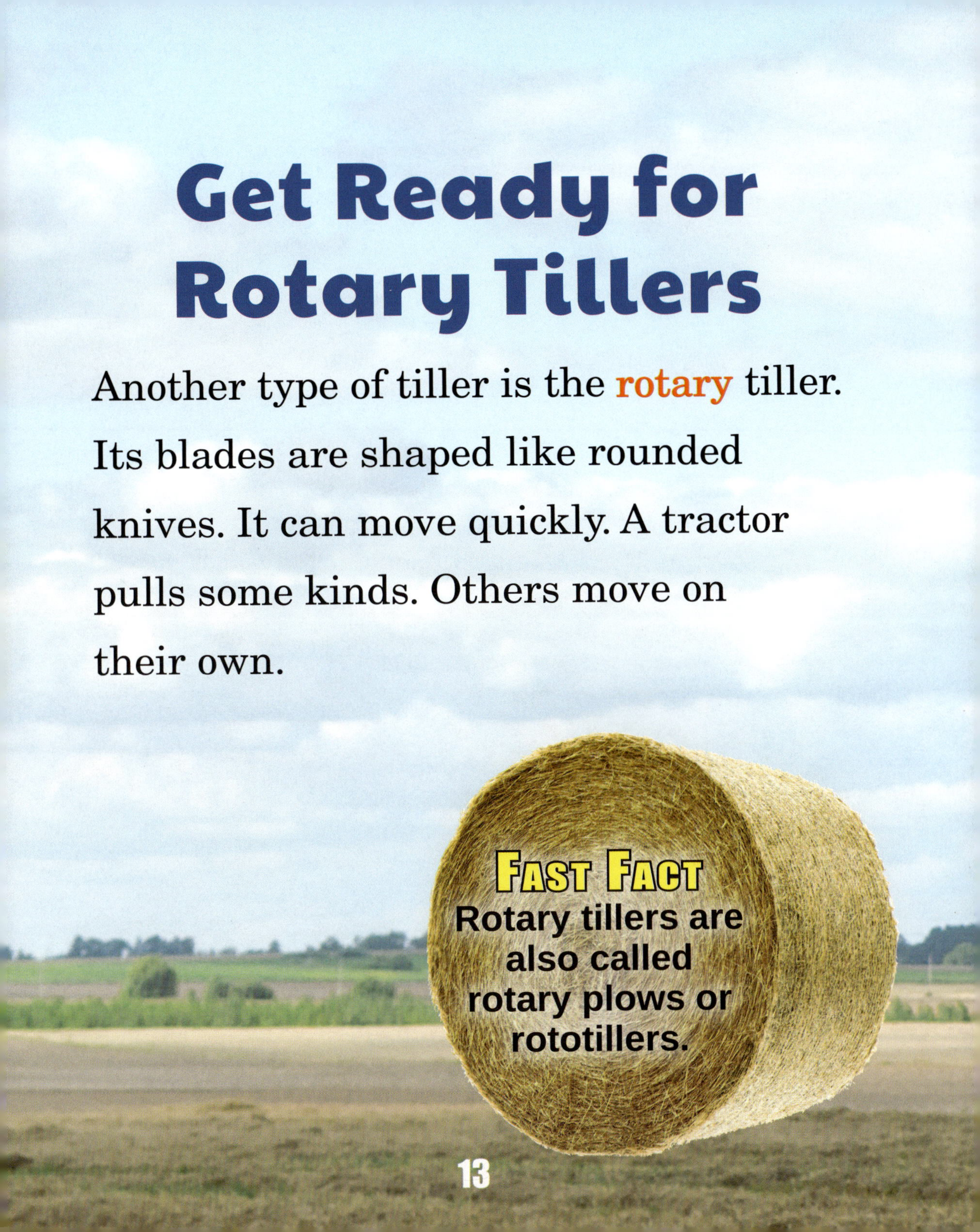

Get Ready for Rotary Tillers

Another type of tiller is the **rotary** tiller. Its blades are shaped like rounded knives. It can move quickly. A tractor pulls some kinds. Others move on their own.

FAST FACT

Rotary tillers are also called rotary plows or rototillers.

This field has been tilled and is ready for seeds.

Types of Tilling

Different farmers want different kinds of soil. It depends on what they are planting. Most want a smooth, flat soil for their seeds. Others want raised rows. They plant on top.

Fast Fact

The spaces between raised rows can help water the crops.

A tiller cuts down cornstalks after the corn has been harvested.

Break It Down

Tillers are for more than soil. After corn is harvested, fields have tough stalks. Sharp blades on tillers break through the cornstalks. They chop them up. They then blend them into the soil.

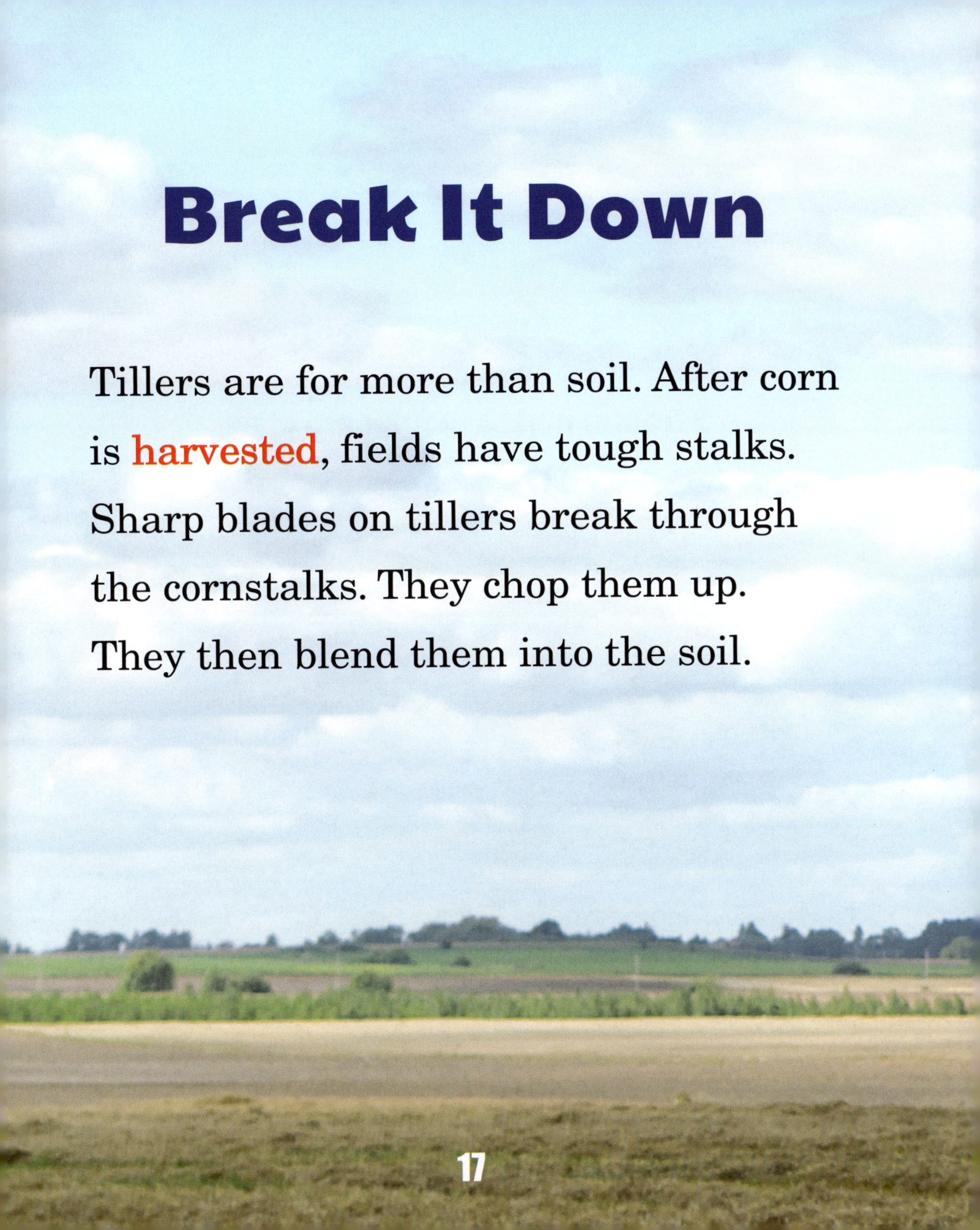

A tractor pulls a moldboard plow.

Meet the Moldboard

Moldboards are simple plows. They go deep into the soil for a first till. Moldboards cut trenches into the dirt. They also move the soil. What started out on top is moved underneath.

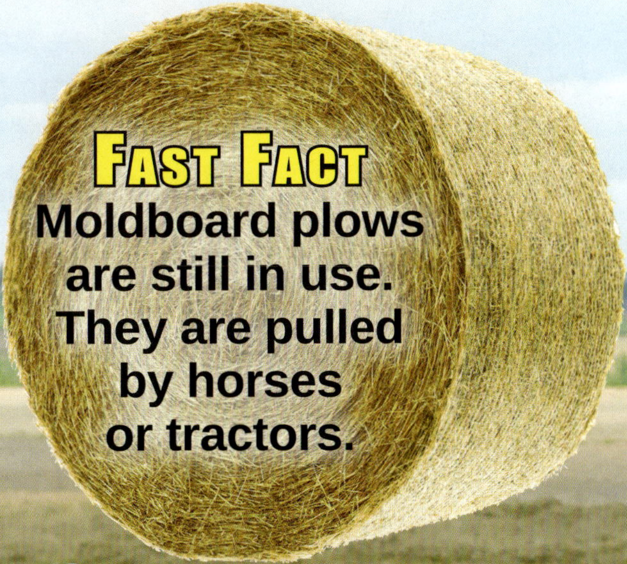

FAST FACT

Moldboard plows are still in use. They are pulled by horses or tractors.

A moldboard plow helps to keep soil healthy and kill weeds and pests.

Parts and Pieces

The moldboard has three basic parts. The sharp share cuts through the soil. The moldboard is above it. It turns and chops the soil. The landside keeps the plow steady.

Activity

Stick To It!

Let's dig in!

You will need:

- Sticks (different sizes)
- Hard soil
- Hoe (optional)

Step 1: Poke your stick at the ground. Is it easy to dig up the dirt?

Step 2: Try different sized sticks. Which size makes it easier?

Step 3: Ask an adult to sharpen the end of your stick. How does it change digging?

Step 4: If your family has a hoe, try that. How does the blade help?

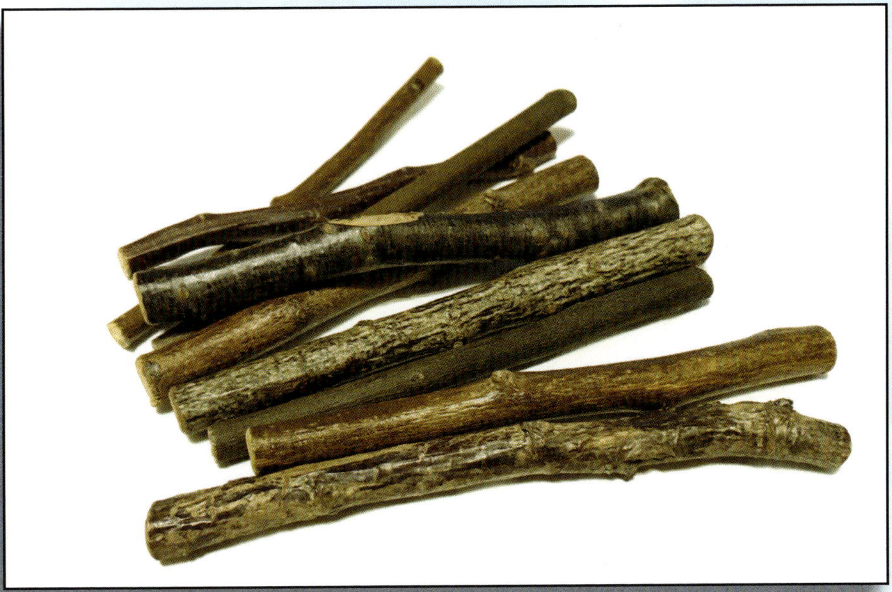

Try using a few different sticks to see which is best for digging up soil.

Learn More

Books

Boothroyd, Jennifer. *Cultivators Go to Work*. Minneapolis, MN: Lerner, 2018.

Borth, Teddy. *Machines on the Farm*. North Mankato, MN: Capstone Classroom, 2016.

Dufek, Holly. *Planters & Cultivators with Casey & Friends*. Austin, TX: Octane Press, 2016.

Website

Plowing with a John Deere 402 Disc Plow
www.youtube.com/watch?v=bVkIvM6NuuI
Check out tools and tools used in tilling.

Index

For Corvus.

Published in 2020 by Enslow Publishing, LLC.
101 W. 23rd Street, Suite 240, New York, NY 10011

Library of Congress Cataloging-in-Publication Data

Names: Niver, Heather Moore, author.
Title: Tilling equipment / author: Heather Moore Niver.
Description: New York : Enslow Publishing, 2020. | Series: Let's learn about farm machines | Includes bibliographical references and index. | Audience: Grades K-3.
Identifiers: LCCN 2019016990| ISBN 9781978513235 (library bound) | ISBN 9781978513211 (pbk.) | ISBN 9781978513228 (6 pack)
Subjects: LCSH: Tillage--Juvenile literature. | Agricultural machinery--Juvenile literature.
Classification: LCC S604 .N548 2020 | DDC 631.3--dc23
LC record available at https://lccn.loc.gov/2019016990

Printed in the United States of America

To Our Readers: We have done our best to make sure all website addresses in this book were active and appropriate when we went to press. However, the author and the publisher have no control over and assume no liability for the material available on those websites or on any websites they may link to. Any comments or suggestions can be sent by email to customerservice@enslow.com.

Photos Credits: Cover, p. 1 smereka/Shutterstock.com; interior pages background landscape Jurgis Mankauskas/Shutterstock.com; p. 4 Constantinis/E+/Getty Images; pp. 5, 7, 9, 11, 13, 15, 17, 19, 22 (hay bale) photomaster/Shutterstock.com; p. 6 © iStockphoto.com/GCammarata; p. 8 Hulton Archive/Getty Images; p. 10 © iStockphoto.com/MihailDechev; p. 12 Ed Buziak/Alamy Stock Photo; p. 14 Ghischeforever/Shutterstock.com; p. 16 © iStockphoto.com/dimid_86; p. 18 Rick Dalton/Passage/Getty Images; p. 20 © iStockphoto.com/Tetiana Garkusha; p. 23 kumacore/Moment/Getty Images; cover, p. 1 logo element (tractor) Krivosheev Vitaly/Shutterstock.com.